People everywhere
ponder the basic question,

"Where did I come from?"

So where do I fit into God's plan?

God's
BIG PICTURE

Finding Yourself in God's Plan

by LaDonna C. Osborn

God's Big Picture:Finding Yourself in God's Plan
ISBN 0-87943-114-8
Copyright © 2001 by LaDonna C. Osborn
Printed in the United States of America.
All Rights Reserved.

OSBORN
PUBLISHERS

Published by Osborn Publishers
P.O. Box 10, Tulsa, OK 74102 USA

Osborn International
P.O. Box 10, Tulsa, OK 74102 USA
918-743-6231 • FAX 918-749-0339
Email: OSFO@aol.com • www.osborn.org

Canada: Box 281, Adelaide St. Post Sta., Toronto M5C 2J4
England: Box 148, Birmingham B3 2LG (a registered charity)

Preview
OF THE GOSPEL

SCENE ONE:
God's Creation

SCENE TWO:
Satan's Deception

SCENE THREE:
Christ's Substitution

The medallion-like graphic displayed in this book
symbolizes the unfolding panorama
of *God's Big Picture*—the gospel—without words.

This icon portrays the four scenes of the gospel drama.
The tree of life represents *God's Creation*.
The serpent evokes *Satan's Deception*.
The cross portrays *Christ's Substitution*.
Finally, the new blossom signifies *Our Restoration*.

The vine as the souce of life,
wraps itself around the whole story,
as does the love of God,
from beginning to end,
in His eternal plan of redemption.

This book is dedicated to
the cherished memory of my mother,

Dr. Daisy
Washburn Osborn,

LaDonna Osborn
    Daisy Washburn Osborn

who formed my
earliest concepts of the
loving eternal Parent.
She demonstrated,
through her consistent
and courageous living,
that the Word of God
still takes on flesh through
Christ's followers who are
willing to make it their energizing force. Dr. Daisy was
my most ardent encourager, my most trusted friend,
my most Christ-centered counselor, and my most
admired role model.

When my mother could have remained surrounded
by the security and comfort of American living, she
chose to go with my father, Dr. T. L. Osborn, to the
ends of the earth proclaiming the Gospel of Jesus Christ
to millions who had never known His love. I was by her
side through so many of her adventures and challenges,
witnessing the power of God in action. Her choice to go
defined my childhood experience, exposing me to the
people of practically every culture and religion of the
world and equipping me for international diplomacy
and gospel ministry.

My mother introduced me to Jesus Christ. Her
example motivated me to follow Him as my supreme
Model and to live by His biblical principles that transcend
culture, tradition and gender. She was a bold herald of
freedom for women and men who were shackled by

myriad forms of spiritual and social bondage. She did what many say a woman cannot do. The arguments of those who limit women are, to me, rendered void because what they say a woman cannot do, Mama *did!* She blazed a trail in biblical Christian ministry that is enabling thousands of others to respond to Christ's call and to follow Him.

Dr. Daisy Washburn Osborn, who transcended her earthly life on May 27, 1995, remains alive through me, as her natural seed, and through tens of thousands of others, as her spiritual seed—daughters and sons around the world who still call her, "Mama."

Special thanks are given to those whose participation and encouragement have made this book a present reality.

My husband, Cory Nickerson, patiently scripted fifty-two audio recordings of my live teachings on redemption, placing in my hands a formidable stack of material that he said was "good stuff."

My agent, Stacie Jennings, insisted that the presentation of the gospel in this four-scene panorama would effectively communicate vital truth to both Christians and non-Christians. I told her that church leaders around the world were begging me for this book; Russian and Chinese translators were already selected. Stacie said, "America needs your message, too."

My friend, Dr. Kelley Varner, assumed the exhausting task of reducing the original fifty-two lessons to a manageable script. His labor and counsel encouraged me to press forward.

My friends, George and Woodie Terrell, are living witnesses to the power and validity of the gospel presented in this book. After more than twenty years of legalistic, debasing and fraudulent religious experience, they "saw" *God's Big Picture*, believed it, and began sharing it with others. They have reminded me, on the phone, via e-mail, in person, through correspondence, and with many remarkable testimonials, that this book will bring hope and solution to people. They worked many hours to insure the accuracy of Bible references, for which I am deeply grateful.

My faithful colleague and friend, Dr. Chyanna Mull-Anthony, endured my moods of discouragement each time another international ministry engagement forced me to return this manuscript to its place among other "pending" projects. She encouraged me to find a secluded location, with no telephones or other distractions, and to complete this book. She absorbed the criticism of those who complained when I did not return calls or was absent from my church pulpit, allowing me to give priority to this task.

My father, Dr. T. L. Osborn, interrupted his own ministry and writing projects to emphasize the importance of placing gospel books in the hands of people, as seed that procreates. He read and re-read my drafts, making valuable suggestions that have improved clarity in what I have written. He would say, "Honey, what you know of the Bible and what you have seen demonstrated among suffering people of so many nations is the message that will change your world. What you preach may be forgotten, but what you write will live and procreate until Christ returns."

Finally, special thanks to our Osborn International Ministry staff, especially Sam Osborn and Billie Mantooth, who have labored with my parents and with me in gospel ministry for many years, and whose publication expertise has been invaluable in the final presentation of this gospel classic.

Redemption
is the biblical theme of the Gospel.

T.L. Osborn   LaDonna Osborn

It is what Christ commissioned the Church and every believer to communicate. It is the revelation of why divine life from God can now be imparted to human persons.

In writing this book, Dr. LaDonna Osborn has painted a four-scene panorama of what constitutes the gospel—of what redemption *is*. I believe this classic volume provides the most vital concept possible to project into the minds of clergy and laity alike— worldwide.

In my long experience both at home and abroad, I have been deeply concerned that so few voices proclaim the fundamental facts of the gospel that constituted Paul's consuming revelation of redemption—so few seem to perceive these basics today as integral and indispensable to faith in God.

Why do we remember names like Calvin, Luther, Wesley, Whitfield, Finney, Spurgeon, and Moody? Because they were gospel preachers. Their messages and ministries were grounded in redemptive truth that was, to them, a living, burning revelation.

There were thousands of other preachers during those epochs. Why do we not remember them? Because their messages were peripheral. The good news of redemption was not a life-changing revelation to them so it was not prioritized in their ministries and they have been forgotten.

The author of this book is passionate about communicating the biblical facts of the gospel. It is the predominant focus of her ministry, as it was for the Apostle Paul. Revealing redemption to people is her priority in ministry. It is the reason for this book—and it is why these pages will engender life-changing influences until Christ returns.

The gospel is the good news of redemption. If it is not enunciated, it will not be understood. If it is not understood, it will not be believed. Unless it is believed, human persons will not be saved. The gospel … *is* the power of God to salvation … [1]

Paul asks, *How shall they believe in Him of whom they have not heard? And how shall they hear without a preacher [or a communicator]?* [2]

If the facts that comprise God's redemption of humanity are not made clear, people may embrace some form of religious Christianity without ever experiencing the fullness of salvation. They may be loyal church members, yet live in insecurity, and remain vulnerable to deception and condemnation by the enemy.

Four epochal scenes depict the panorama of the gospel that Dr. LaDonna Osborn presents here—*Creation, Deception, Substitution,* and *Restoration.* They comprise the essence of what the Bible is all about. *God's Big Picture* is written to focus the significance of these four biblical events, and to reveal how they transform the reader as soon as they are embraced.

Once one understands these four facts, the Bible makes sense. Believing and embracing them is what we call faith—saving and healing faith that is created in one's heart by simply comprehending the essence of redemptive facts. That is the aim of this book.

People often want to know the secret of the long success of the Osborn World Ministries. It is that we consistently communicate the essence of the four biblical facts elucidated in this book.

Dr. LaDonna Osborn embraces these essential gospel facts as the essence of her most cherished and most consequential revelation. They constitute the why of her unbending faith and the reason for her mission to millions in this generation.

God's Big Picture portrays the grand panorama of redemption. Christian ministers have preached and written biblical truths for centuries. None that I have known about has compacted the essence of the gospel in such a simple, yet forceful, four-scene framework as is presented here.

I urge gospel ministers, teachers, and students to ponder the significance of these scenes until, like the Apostle Paul, you will be *determined to not know anything among people except Jesus Christ, and Him crucified;* [and until your] *speech and preaching* [will not] *be with persuasive words of human wisdom, but in demonstration of the Spirit and of power; so that* [the people's] *faith should not be in* [human] *wisdom, but in the power of God.*[3]

I urge believers to ponder these simple, yet pivotal scenes that comprise the essence of the gospel, until, like the Apostle Paul, you will resolve to never allow your mind to be *corrupted from the simplicity that is in Christ.*[4]

We now belong to a new millennium—a new century. May this graphic book seed a clear understanding and birth a fresh renaissance of biblical simplicity in grasping what the essence of the gospel is.

Nations of the world previously closed to the gospel are imminently opening to the message of Christ.

The author of this book recently returned from

3. I Corinthians 2:2-5   4. 2 Corinthians 11:3

a period of intense ministry in China, preaching five times each day during her entire mission. She dedicated tons of our books that are now published in Mandarin and are being circulated through over eight thousand underground preaching points. She has her eyes on China, on Russia and on the fifteen unevangelized republics of the former Soviet Union. This book is the message of redemption that she is passionately sharing with her world.

In Eurasia, the communist enslavement of people forbade any knowledge of God for more than seventy years. In ten of the greatest cities of the ex-Soviet Union, Dr. LaDonna Osborn has ministered and proclaimed the essence of this book. Hundreds who heard her are already in full-time ministry. The nations of this generation are uninterested in Americanized theology. They want the gospel—in simplicity—in demonstration of the Spirit and of power.

The gospel is what Jesus sent His followers to communicate. The gospel is what He promises to confirm. The gospel is what works—and it will procreate living faith, hope, and love, in human persons until Christ returns.

God's Big Picture is the biblical focus of the gospel.

T.L. Osborn

The content of this book is both amazingly simple and astoundingly profound in significance.

BY LADONNA OSBORN

Preface

The mental images that take form may affect the reader's deepest levels of religious presuppositions, reshaping the way he or she thinks about God, about the world, and about oneself.

This book is not a comprehensive treatise on redemption—it is not intended to be an exhaustive Bible study on the subject. It is an attempt to take the fundamental essentials of biblical faith and focus them as one unfolding panorama of God's plan for people like you and me.

God's Big Picture is the central theme of the biblical text that begins in Genesis and continues through Revelation. The Bible defines God's design for people and it contains the information necessary for the fulfillment of human purpose. It is not a mystery intended for an elite few. It is one magnificent panorama of God's loving plan for all human persons.

The first two chapters of Genesis set forth God's original dream for His creation.

The third chapter of Genesis exposes Satan's scheme to thwart God's plan, and then it announces God's strategy to restore His dream.

Chapters four through eleven of Genesis detail the resulting corruption of God's creation and His resolve to give humankind a new beginning.

The twelfth chapter of Genesis (and continuing throughout the Old Testament) begins the saga of God's redemptive plan for humanity declared in His promises to Abraham and Sarah.

The Book of Exodus is a dramatic picture of God's plan in one historic drama, beginning with the bondage of His people in Egypt and the birth of their deliverer, and ending with the completion of the wilderness Tabernacle, in which God dwells in the midst of His people.

From the remainder of the books of Moses, through the historic writings, the wisdom literature, and the words of the prophets, God speaks to His creation. In historic events; through visuals of worship, ceremonial sacrifices and festivals; and in many ways God reveals Himself as loving Creator and faithful Redeemer. The entire Old Testament can be synopsized as a preview of God's predestined plan to come and redeem His creation, despite repeated disobedience.

The New Testament Gospels of Matthew, Mark, Luke, and John announce the arrival of God's promised Redeemer, Jesus Christ. He fulfills every anticipation of hope and each promise of salvation communicated in the Old Testament. Christ's earthly life and ministry unveil the fulfillment of God's original plan for people.

Subsequent New Testament books, from the Acts of the Apostles to the Book of Jude, are inspiring and instructive accounts about ordinary people responding to God's activity manifested through those who believe in Christ.

The final Bible book of Revelation is written as a captivating word picture of God's ultimate and glorious victory over the adversary, through Christ as both the substitutionary Lamb and as the conquering King.

God's Big Picture presents a synopsis of the principal story of the Bible—the gospel—through the unfolding panorama of four events that allow God's marvelous plan of redemption to become clear and relevant in the lives of women and men who read it.

When *God's Big Picture* is viewed biblically, the results are clarity where there has been confusion, revelation where there has been resistance, peace where there has been perplexity, and solution where there has been strife.

Many Christian books have been written to expound complex theological topics, such as sin or salvation, or to explain common Christian disciplines, such as prayer or perseverance. The purpose of this book is neither to expound nor to explain, but to invite each reader to experience a living faith that will transform his or her life.

What qualifies me to suggest that the realities conveyed in this book can fulfill such daring claims?

It was my good fortune to be raised by parents (Drs. T. L. Osborn and Daisy Washburn Osborn) whose primary mission has been to communicate God's good news to people around the world. The year that I was born (1947), our family began traveling from nation to nation pioneering mass miracle evangelism in non-Christian nations, with the demonstration of supernatural signs and wonders, and inaugurating methods to bring people effectively into a transforming relationship with God through Jesus Christ. The world was literally my playground and children of differing skin colors and cultural lifestyles were my playmates.

During a lifetime of Christian ministry among the peoples of the world, I have learned that biblical truth transcends culture and tradition, and that the gospel must be both declared and demonstrated if it is to be believed and embraced by people who have their own religion, ethnic culture, and national traditions.

As carriers of God's message of hope and love to all people, we must convey the essentials of biblical faith in ways that can be clearly understood.

Redemptive truth is effective in all circumstances

and is for all people, because it concerns God's unchanging plan for His entire human creation.

God's Big Picture is the heart of biblical truth. I have presented this panorama to people around the world in many different ways, using imagery, parables, and pictorial dramatizations to communicate God's plan for the redemption of humankind. What is now published in this book will not engage the reader in the tedious detail of religious argument, but it will elevate the reader to the transcending drama of God's love in action.

This gospel classic is intended to be a discussion, between author and reader, that leads to discovery and an exchange that results in experience. The four fundamental scenes of this book, depicting *God's Big Picture*, are the biblical truths that can replace the pious ritual of religion with the practical relevance of relationship.

God's Big Picture introduces a faith that is factual, not mystical. It presents absolutes that are enduring, not faddish. Through this gospel panorama, you can discover yourself in God's plan.

LaDonna C. Osborn

Preview
OF THE GOSPEL

This book presents
a panoramic perspective
of the Bible,

of God's original design

for people,

and of His resolve

to never abandon

His plan for their good.

*I*t emphasizes how much God believes in human persons, despite their faults, and how much He has invested to restore them to Himself as His partners in life. It unveils the grand drama of His grace and love that makes it possible for people to experience His life that brings renewed dignity, vital equality, and dynamic purpose to their daily living. This, in essence, is what we call the *Gospel of Redemption*.

THE GOSPEL OF REDEMPTION

Redemption is the foundation of all spiritual revelation.

Perceiving the drama of human redemption is the key that unlocks biblical truth.

The truths of redemption convey the message that offers hope and dignity to humanity. God's redemption of humankind

To understand redemption is to glimpse the heart of God.

is the biblical solution to life's perplexing questions.

The story of redemption unveils the panorama of the Creator's love in action. It is *God's Big Picture.*

To understand redemption is to glimpse the heart of God. The gospel, the *power of God to salvation,*[1] is the only message the Church is commissioned to proclaim.[2] The facts of redemption express what Jesus accomplished on the cross, reveal why it was necessary for

Redemption is the basis for balanced and buoyant Christian living.

Him to sacrifice His life on our behalf, and disclose who we are as human beings because of God's redemptive action.

Comprehending redemptive truth is the basis for confident and consistent faith in God, and for balanced and buoyant Christian living. Embracing these principles of redemption stabilizes and vitalizes the believer's thinking. Putting them into practice in daily living is what validates our witness of Christ in our world.

---

1. Romans 1:16   2. Mark 16:15

FOUR SCENES
COMPRISE ONE PICTURE

The panorama of *God's Big Picture* is a progressive story of the fulfillment of His beautiful plan for humanity. It portrays four significant events that together comprise the essence of biblical truth. These events are sequential. They may be studied separately but only as they are interwoven and viewed as one continuum can the knowledge of redemption transform the lives of people.

These four dynamic events of redemption are:

    1) God's *Creation*,

    2) Satan's *Deception*,

    3) Christ's *Substitution*, and

    4) our *Restoration*.

These four fundamentals begin in the Book of Genesis and unfold throughout the Scriptures. They express the purpose of God's creative plan, expose the deception of the enemy, expound the redemptive work of Christ, and explain His restorative presence in each person who embraces them.

This redemptive revelation brings:

Dignity for the demeaned,

Forgiveness to the condemned,

Beauty to the blemished,

Confidence to the frustrated,

Comfort to the bereaved,

Virtue to the depraved,

Direction to the confused,

Faith to the unbelieving,

Self-esteem to the disparaged,

Integrity to the fraudulent,

Nobility to the outcast,

Distinction to the ordinary,

Restoration to the alienated,

Power to the weak,

Health to the diseased,

Strength to the weary,

Freedom to the captive,

Security to the vulnerable,

Hope to the despairing, and

Life to the dying.

REDEMPTION IS A MIRACLE

For I am not ashamed of the Gospel of Christ, for it is the power of God to salvation for everyone who believes...[3]

So, if anyone is in Christ, there is a new creation; everything old has passed away; see, everything has become new. All this is from God, who reconciles us to himself through Christ, and has given us the ministry of reconciliation; that is, in Christ God was reconciling the world to Himself, not counting their trespasses against them, and entrusting the message of reconciliation to us. So we are ambassadors for Christ, since God is making His appeal through us; we entreat you on behalf of Christ, be reconciled to God. For our sake he made him to be sin who knew no sin, so that in him we might become the righteousness of God.[4]

This is redemption. It covers the full intervention of God that reconciles us to Him in Christ, and that enables us to represent Him to others. This new creation miracle is only made possible through the redeeming work of Jesus. He is the central character in the drama of redemption—*God's Big Picture.*

---

3. Romans 1:16   4. 2 Corinthians 5:17-21 (New Revised Standard Version).

The gospel is the overall perspective of four major facts: 1) God created us; 2) Satan tried to destroy us; 3) Jesus redeemed us; and 4) we are now reconciled and restored to God as His friends and representatives.

With this focused biblical vista, these four events form an interpretive overlay of the Bible, making its design clear, and revealing our own identity, dignity, and divine purpose in life.

The gospel—or redemption—is good news and it is for everyone. *Whoever calls upon the name of the Lord shall be saved.*[5] *For God took the sinless Christ and poured into him our sins. Then, in exchange, he poured God's goodness into us!*[6]

Jesus is the central character in redemption's drama.

To redeem means:

1. To buy back; to repurchase.

2. To get back; to recover, as by paying a fee.

3. To pay off (a mortgage or note).

4. To rescue, ransom, or liberate from captivity or bondage, or from any liability or obligation to suffer.

5. Acts 2:21   6. 2 Corinthians 5:21 (The Living Bible).

5. To deliver, rescue, save in any manner.

6. To perform, as a promise; to make good by performance.

7. To make amends for; to atone for, to compensate.

8. In law, to recall, as an estate, or to regain, as mortgaged property, by payment of what may be due according to the terms of the mortgage.

9. In theology, to deliver from sin and its penalties, as by a substitute assuming the guilt and enduring the judgment assigned to the sinner.

GOSPEL—THE KEY TO THE BIBLE

God's redemption of humankind, through Christ, reinstates us to our rightful place with Him and restores us as His representatives in the world,

God redeems us to our rightful place with Him.

enabling us to fulfill our predestined purpose. This is the central theme in the Scriptures of God's revealed design and will for us.

Therefore, I re-emphasize that the knowledge of redemption is the foundation of all spiritual revelation. Christian doctrine is to be evaluated by and be consistent with the underlying and overarching revelation of the gospel of redemption.

An unwavering confidence is produced in those whose faith is based on redemptive truth. It produces assurance in the believer's…

> …knowledge of God,
>
> …relationship with God,
>
> …personal value to God,
>
> …power and authority over Satan, and
>
> …divine purpose in God's Kingdom..

Drs. T. L. and Daisy Osborn, my parents, have crisscrossed this planet together for more than a half-century, always expounding for multitudes these four basic redemptive issues that comprise the gospel.[7]

1. *God's Creation*—humanity's origin in God.

2. *Satan's Deception*—the beginning of human suffering.

3. *Christ's Substitution*—His death and resurrection on our behalf

4. *Our Restoration*—the reality of God's life expressed in and through us as believers today.

---

7. T.L. Osborn, *The Message that Works* (Tulsa, OK: OSFO Books, 1997), 18,20.

The gospel of redemption is the good news that every man and woman can believe in Jesus Christ as his or her Redeemer and Lord and can begin living His victorious lifestyle now. For all who believe, redemption is a present reality, and Satan is already defeated. Christ's victory is their victory, and His righteousness is now theirs.[8]

Redemption is a present reality

God's Big Picture begins on the first page of the Book of Genesis and continues through the last page of the Book of Revelation. It is this one plan, this glorious unfolding panorama, and this progressive revelation of God's love, that we call redemption. Through it, we can know God and discover His magnificent plan.

I have proclaimed this good news in nations around the world, on open fields, in coliseums, in ballparks, and in large and small churches. This gospel has been announced from my lips in every imaginable ambiance, from ornate pulpits of elaborate cathedrals, and from the tops of wooden boxes in the center of public village markets.

Wherever the announcement of God's redemptive

8. Ibid., 359

plan is heralded with clarity and relevance, the results are the same. Lives are changed by His power and healing miracles confirm that *Jesus Christ is the same yesterday, today and forever.*[9] His gospel is the power of God.[10]

Church leaders and Bible teachers often neglect the dynamic revelation of redemption that was the driving passion of the Apostle Paul's ministry. Contemporary Christians often popularize secondary issues, giving minimal attention to the biblical facts of redemption. Pastoral themes such as prayer, fasting, gifts of the Spirit, prosperity, healing, marriage, ethics, etc., must be presented within the essential framework of the revelation of redemption. It is the *a priori* principle of Scripture by which all biblical doctrine is measured. It is vital that we comprehend the redemptive reasons why God's provisions and His power are available to us as believers in Christ.

Only the gospel of Christ's redemption has power to produce lasting change.

Popular, trendy teachings come and go. Only the gospel of Christ's redemption produces enduring change in

9. Hebrews 13:8   10. Romans 1:16

human lives. The good news of redemption is as effective in the villages of interior Africa as among the sophisticates of Japan. It is as miraculously productive in Papua New Guinea as it is in England, Canada, or the United States. Why? Because *the Gospel is the power of God*,[11] regardless of the social culture, the religious tradition, or the economic or academic level of the people to whom it is presented. Everyone deserves to hear the gospel, so that each can believe it and be saved, healed, and enjoy purposeful living.[12] The mission of clergy and laity alike is to communicate the gospel to our world.

To understand this gospel of redemption we will now focus on each of the four significant scenes that comprise *God's Big Picture*, beginning with His *Creation*.

---

11. Romans 1:16   12. Romans 10:13-15

SCENE ONE
God's Creation

*The first scene
of God's Big Picture
occurs in the Garden of Eden,
at the dawn of creation.*

The first two chapters
of the Book of Genesis are
much more than historic accounts
of how the world began.

They reveal God as the Creator,
and disclose the purpose for which
everything was created.

ur study of the gospel must begin in Genesis. If *God's Big Picture* of redemption includes our restoration, to what condition, status, or lifestyle are we restored? What was His divine plan in the beginning? Why did God create human persons and what was His dream for us? How is it achieved? Knowing God's plan for people in the beginning, prepares us to comprehend His plan for us today.

Knowing God's plan in the beginning prepares us to comprehend His plan for us today.

In the beginning God created the heavens and the earth.[1]

Everything that the Master Designer created had a purpose. The heavens were created to provide seasons for the earth.[2] The earth was created for habitation by humankind.[3] Within this planet, God stored every mineral, chemical, nutrient, treasure, and resource that humanity could ever need. People were created to be in relationship with God as their Father.[4]

---

1. Genesis 1:1   2. Genesis 1:14   3. Isaiah 45:18   4. Ephesians 1:4; 3:14-15

Then God said, Let Us make man [humankind]
in Our image, according to Our likeness; let them have dominion
over the fish of the sea, over the birds of the air, and over the
cattle, over all the earth and over every creeping thing that creeps
on the earth. Therefore, God created man [humankind] in His
own image; in the image of God He created him; male and
female He created them.[5]

THE IMAGE OF GOD-
DESIGN FOR HUMAN DIGNITY

The Creator said, Let us make people. This indicates
great deliberation and forethought. Humankind alone, among
all the creatures,
is capable of
sustained
thought,
creativity, and
the awareness
of God.

> *Humankind alone,*
> *among all creatures, is capable*
> *of sustained thought, creativity,*
> *and the awareness of God.*

The phrase *according to Our likeness* implies understanding
and intellect. Animals were given instincts that motivate their

activities, but God conferred upon people the gift of thought, moral choice, the ability to do right or wrong, and to obey or disobey.[6] In this freedom, we glimpse one of the characteristics of the divine image and likeness that distinguishes humanity from lower created beings.

Why did God create humanity with such lofty and noble abilities? The Scripture teaches us that *God is love.*[7] Love requires expression. Love takes initiative. Love fashioned the earth to be humanity's garden of discovery wherein man and woman would experience the goodness of their Creator, explore the wonders of relationship with Him, and express His life and presence in the earth.

The most ennobling and dignifying attribute of humankind is that as human beings, we are the offspring

The most dignifying fact in human history is that as humans we are the offspring of God.

of God. People everywhere ponder the basic question, "Where did we come from?" For instance, Papua New Guinea tribespeople imagine that they came from alligators.

---

6. See Luke 9:23-25,62; John 14:21-23; Romans 6:16; Hebrews 5:9   7. 1 John 4:8

Scene One of *God's Big Picture* establishes that human origin is rooted in God. He created people in His image for relationship and for purpose. Human dignity is established by the God-image that is stamped upon every individual.

Through my imagination, I can see the sovereign God begin to paint

> *Human dignity is established by the God image stamped upon every person.*

the deliberate and premeditated picture of redemption against the backdrop of eternity. He brushes the landscape with loving detail, careful to include copious shades of color and lavish dimensions of texture. Fanning breezes animate the magnificent trees and the numerous flowers that emit exquisite fragrances. Streams splash and sparkle. Mountains rise majestically into the mist. God walks and talks with the man and woman whom He fashioned in His own likeness. The beautiful garden scene is complete. Everything is perfect. Adam is handsome. Eve is beautiful. They are strong and happy—perfect human specimens. They are neither disabled nor deficient. They are not disgruntled or depressed. All is well in God's original creation.

The Psalmist David expressed in awe: *What are human beings, that you are mindful of them, mortals that you care for them? You have made them a little lower than God, and crowned them with glory and honor. You have given them dominion over the works of your hands; you have put all things under their feet ...*[8]

It is essential that we see ourselves as God *originally* designed us, as His offspring—His divine reflections on the earth. He created us a little lower than Himself,[9] in His own image and likeness. Humankind was created in God's class of being, with special abilities—not animals, but as God-like creations, purposefully endowed with divine dignity.

> *Humankind was created in God's class of being, with special abilities.*

---

8. Psalms 8:4-6 (NRSV)   9. The Hebrew word *elohim*, sometimes translated as "the angels" in Psalm 8:5, is the name used for God in the first five chapters of the Book of Genesis.

MALE AND FEMALE—
CREATED FOR EQUALITY

God committed to humankind, *both* to male and
female, the care of everything that He had created.[10] He
breathed His life into
them, filling them with
His presence and
equipping them for
partnership and for
union and communion

*In God's initial design,
the man and the woman
were equal.*

with Him.[11] God blessed *both* Adam and Eve. He gave
instructions to them *both*. He entrusted dominion over His
creation to them *both*.[12] Adam and Eve *both* walked with
Him in the garden, in the cool of the day.[13] In God's initial
design, the man and the woman were equal, and were one in
fellowship and in friendship with their Creator.

GOD'S "ONE FLESH" PATTERN

The more detailed account of creation, in the second
chapter of Genesis, emphasizes the forming of Eve and the

---

10. Genesis 1:27-28   11. Genesis 2:7   12. Genesis 1:28   13.Genesis 3:8

joining of Adam and Eve as one flesh. Remember that they were both made in the image of God. It is fundamental that we understand the triune nature of God (God the Father, God the Son, and God the Holy Spirit)—plurality expressed in perfect unity. Humanity is created to express this same unity.

The Scripture teaches that it is *not good for man to be alone*.[14] Adam, alone, did not reflect the full image of God. God took a part of Adam with which He formed Eve. In this significant action, we observe the essential oneness and shared identity of humanity. Out of Adam, Eve was fashioned. Adam and Eve (representing all of humanity) became one flesh and completed God's expression of His own image and likeness—of His plurality expressed in unity.[15] The interdependence and unity of male and female is further underscored by the fact that from the union of both Adam and Eve, offspring were produced.

It is significant to notice that Eve was formed to be a helper for the specific purpose of delivering Adam from his singularity.[16] Certain erroneous interpretations of Genesis 2:18 insist that the female was predetermined by God to be inferior to the male, and to fulfill a role that is subservient. That is inconsistent with God's plan for humanity as revealed in Scripture.

---

14. Genesis 2:18   15. Genesis 2:24   16. Genesis 2:18

The Hebrew word *ezer* (e-zer') (sometimes translated *helper*) is used throughout the Old Testament— primarily in reference to God.[17] The word *ezer* certainly does not imply inferiority. God is not inferior to those whom He helps. The word *ezer*, used in describing God's intent in forming Eve was never meant to diminish her dignity nor to alter the purpose for which both men and women were created.

> *God's intent in forming Eve was not to diminish the dignity for which both men and women were created.*

Most societies do not place the same value on females as they do on males. Unfortunately, many Christians overlay the biblical text with their own biases and societal norms. Understanding God's redemptive plan exposes the deep-rooted cause of the usual struggle that exists between men and women and that results in the subjugation of females. God's created standard of equality can only be realized when people embrace the principles of biblical redemption.

---

17. Examples: 1 Samuel 7:12; Psalm 121:1-2

THE GOD OF PURPOSE
CREATED PEOPLE OF PURPOSE

God created humankind—both men and women—to live together in unity and in harmony with Him and with each other. Together they are to be His representatives in the earth. This *dignity*, *equality*, and divine *purpose* are restored through knowledge of the gospel and by comprehending *God's Big Picture*.

Then God blessed them, and God said to them, "Be fruitful and multiply; fill the earth and subdue it; have dominion over the fish of the sea, over the birds of the air, and over every living thing that moves on the earth."[18]

God's Creation—His plan for humankind—includes the element of *purpose*. Adam and Eve were told to be fruitful and multiply. Inherent in this command is the reality that humanity is endowed with God-given procreative ability. He created the first man and woman and entrusted to them the power to reproduce other Godlike beings. The spiritual significance of this human responsibility and purpose will be discussed in a later chapter.

---

18. Genesis 1:28

God instructed both Adam and Eve to subdue
the earth and to have dominion over His creation. Inherent
in this command is the reality that both men and women are
endowed with God-given authority to rule and to have authority.

The purpose of this chapter is to clearly identify the
original plan
for humankind
as it is etched
in beautiful
detail in *God's
Creation*. In
the garden,

> *God created the first
> man and woman and then
> entrusted to them the power to
> reproduce other Godlike beings.*

1. Male and female were created in the *dignity* of God's
   image and likeness.

2. Male and female were created with unique abilities.

3. Male and female were created with superiority over the
   rest of God's creation.

4. Male and female were created for *equality*.

5. Male and female were created to be expressions and
   representatives of God.

6. Male and female were created to reproduce Godlike
   beings.

---

1 Revelation 13:8 2 See John 1:1-4, 14; Ephesians 1:7; Colossians 1:13-14;
Hebrews 4:5; I Peter 2:24; I John 2:2

7. Male and female were created with authority to rule.

8. Male and female were created to be God's partners and
to share His *purpose*.

*Then God saw everything that He had made, and
indeed it was very good.*[19]

Understanding God's original plan is the only basis
for true self-esteem. This is what enables the human person
to fulfill his or her
divinely predestined
purpose. God's love
and esteem for people
determine their
worth. Our attitude

*God's love and
esteem for people determine
human worth.*

toward people should reflect God's attitude toward them.
Our value of people should reflect God's value of them. It is
right to esteem what He values. Feelings of inferiority and
jealousy will be transformed into personal confidence with
the realization that we are created with divine DNA, designed
for God's divine purpose.

*For we are His workmanship, created in Christ Jesus
for good works.*[20]

---

19. Genesis 1:31   20. Ephesians 2:10

Humankind was created to be in relationship with God and with each other as one human family.[21] This divine connection and reflection of God's nature in humankind is the substance of the first scene of *God's Big Picture*. It is here that human dignity, equality, and purpose are established.

SPIRIT-POWER–
INVESTED IN HUMANITY

Before we consider the events that cast a death shadow upon the canvas of *God's Big Picture*, we must first identify the source of the power that marred God's image in humankind.

Genuine power is spiritual. The unseen world of the spirit is more real than the seen world of our physical senses. The writer of Hebrews expresses it this way, *By faith we understand that the worlds were framed by the word of God, so that the things which are seen were not made of things which are visible.*[22] The Spirit of God, which is unseen, created the world, which is seen. All real power emanates from a spirit source. God is Spirit, with no beginning and no ending;[23] Satan is spirit, a created being.[24] Human persons are spirits,

---

21. John 17; Ephesians 3:14-15   22. Hebrews 11:3   23. John 4:24   24. Ephesians 2:2

created in the image of God.[25] All real power is spiritual.

The material world reflects in tangible form the realities existent in the spiritual world. Though we live in a physical body, we are essentially spiritual beings made in the image of God who is Spirit.[26] Our unseen spirits animate our physical bodies. While we relate to this physical world through our natural senses, we relate to the invisible world of spirit through our spiritual senses.[27]

Our spirits were designed for continual, life-sustaining union with God. We were not created to live separate from Him. Everything about the human

We were not created for separation from God but for relationship with Him.

person is designed for and naturally craves this spiritual connection and sense of identification with the Creator.

God did not force Himself on His human creation. He endowed Adam and Eve with the power of choice, allowing them to choose whether or not to remain in relationship with Him.

So, what happened to this *very good*[28] creation where

---

25. Genesis 1:26; 2:7   26. Genesis 1:26-27; compare 1 Thessalonians 5:23; Hebrews 12:9
27. Romans 1:20; 2 Corinthians 4:1,18; Hebrews 5:14   28. Genesis 1:31

Adam and Eve lived in harmony with each other and with
God, where they were joined together in *dignity*, *equality* and
purpose, and where God's life flowed freely to and through
His beautiful human creation?

SCENE TWO
Satan's Deception

*The panorama of
God's Big Picture
includes a scene so grim
that we prefer to
look away.*

Something so catastrophic happens

that only God Himself

can offer the redeeming solution.

menacing shadow settles over the beauty and purity of God's living presence with His man and woman. Alienation replaces relationship. Fear replaces courage. Disease replaces health. Turmoil replaces peace. Deficiency replaces abundance. Shame replaces dignity. Division replaces unity. Separation replaces equality. Segregation of social classes, the domination of man over woman, of the wealthy over the poor, of the strong over the weak and all such inequities replace the loving mutual interdependence that the human family enjoyed as they walked with God.

Everything that was created to function in harmonious perfection becomes fractured and flawed.

Everything that was created to function in harmonious perfection becomes fractured and flawed. What happened? To understand the scope of God's plan of redemption, we must revisit the Garden of Eden where sin enters the human family, disrupting the balance of equality between Adam and Eve, and disjoining them and their offspring from the sustaining presence of God.

TRUST: THE COHESION
OF RELATIONSHIP

The Bible book of Genesis is the book of *beginnings*.
It contains the record of God's creation of the heavens and the
earth, and of every living thing. It documents the beginning
of the human story. Adam and Eve were made in God's image
and placed in the Garden of Eden that He lovingly designed
for them.[1] He enumerated for them the various living and
seed bearing creations for which they were to care, and by
which they were to be sustained.[2]

*The tree of life was also in the midst of the garden, and the
tree of the knowledge of good and evil.*[3]

*And the Lord God commanded ... Of every tree of the garden
you may freely eat; but of the tree of the knowledge of good and evil
you shall not
eat, for in the
day that you eat
of it you shall
surely die.*[4]

*Love provided options, requiring
Adam and Eve to make choices.*

---

1 Genesis 2:8   2. Genesis 1:1-29   3. Genesis 2:9   4. Genesis 2:16-17

59

Adam and Eve were created with the ability to make moral choices. In doing so, God invested them with great dignity. Love provided options. They could choose to obey or to disobey.

Their choice was fundamentally motivated by their attitude toward God. Was He dependable? Could He be trusted? Could Adam and Eve's lives survive based on commitment to God's plan, or were His interests to be suspect?

The cohesive element that sustained this loving God-people connection was *trust*. That rapport could not be maintained by force or coercion.

> *The God-people connection was sustained by trust, not by force.*

God trusted Adam and Eve with His breath, with His life, and with His word. He trusted them with His nature, with His authority, and with His power of procreation. He trusted man and woman to tend the Garden of Eden, and to care for all that He had created, to populate the earth with Godlike persons, and together to reflect His image.

God's Word to Adam and Eve was the authority by

which their attitudes and actions would be judged. Their trust in God would be evidenced by their obedience to His Word. Adam and Eve were to trust God just as He trusted them. They were to trust His integrity and His goodness. Their absolute trust and dependence on Him would be expressed by their obedience to His Words of instruction.

God's only prohibition for Adam and Eve was to not eat from the tree of the knowledge of good and evil. All else was given to them. They lacked nothing.

Now the serpent was more cunning than any beast of the field which the LORD God had made. And he said to the woman, Has God indeed said, You shall not eat of every tree of the garden?[5]

Then the serpent [contradicted God's Word and] *said to the woman, You will not surely die.*[6]

This serpent, a created being who had rebelled against God,[7] crept into the Garden of Eden to oppose God's purposes on earth. Satan had no supremacy or spiritual power of control over Adam and Eve unless he could induce them to question God's word and to disobey Him.

---

5. Genesis 3:1   6. Genesis 3:4   7. Isaiah 14:12-15; Ezekiel 28:12-17; Luke 10:18

GOD'S INTEGRITY IS QUESTIONED

Satan's strategy was to destroy the harmony that maintained God, Adam, and Eve in perfect union. He attacked the trust that was indispensable to their relationship.

This enemy of God (Satan) deceived Eve by carefully wording his conversation with her, suggesting that trust in God's word was not of importance. When Adam and Eve doubted the truthfulness of what God had said, the flow of His divine life to His human creation was obstructed. Without trust, there could be no relationship, nor can there be today.

Without trust, there can be no relationship.

DEATH—WHAT IS IT?

So when the woman saw that the tree was good for food, that it was pleasant to the eyes, and a tree desirable to make one wise,

*she took of its fruit and ate. She also gave to her husband with
her, and he ate.*[8]

Adam and Eve chose to believe Satan's lie, rather
than to believe God's truth. That was the original sin. *Satan's
deception* dealt a catastrophic blow to humanity by severing
the life-flow between people and God.

*Just as sin came into the world through one man, and death
came through sin, and so death spread to all because all have sinned…*[9]

By one man's disobedience many were made sinners…[10]

For the wages of sin is death.[11]

The moment that Adam and Eve became disengaged
from God's sustaining life, deterioration and death began the
work of physical and spiritual destruction. They chose to doubt
God, to not trust Him. That was sin.[12] Sin separates people
from God.[13] Adam and Eve's lack of trust in God resulted in
their disobedience. The sin of doubt, or mistrust, separated
them—and consequently the entire human race—from God
and from His life. God is the author of life.[14] Where His life is
not present, death reigns.

Satan's deception led to what we call the Fall of
humankind. Separated from God's life, humanity was plunged

---

8. Genesis 3:6   9. Romans 5:12   10. Romans 5:19   11. Romans 6:23
12. Romans 14:23   13. Isaiah 59:2   14. John 1:4; I Timothy 6:13

into the gloom and darkness of death.[15] This insidious infection contaminated the entire human race. The seed of death was engendered, through Adam and Eve, in every member of the human

Where God's life is not present, death reigns.

family. All, therefore, have sinned,[16] and the wage, or the harvest of that sin, is death.[17]

CONSEQUENCES OF SIN

Death is the word used in Scripture to describe three types of separation. First, death is spiritual separation from God. People who are estranged from their Creator and His life are spiritually dead.

Second, death is separation of the body from the spirit.

Third, there is the second death, which is eternal separation from God.[18] Those who pass into eternity without accepting God's invitation to come into relationship with Him experience the second death. After death, there is no further

---

15. Romans 5:17   16. Romans 3:23   17. Romans 3:10,23; compare John 5:24; Romans 5:21; 8:2; Ephesians 2:1   18. Revelation 2:11; 20:6,14; 21:8

opportunity for people to be reunited with their Creator
and to live with Him throughout eternity.

*Whoever has the Son has life; whoever does not have the
Son of God does not have life.*[19]

As we explore the magnitude
of *God's Big Picture* of redemption, we
will show that just as separation from
God brings death, reconciliation to
God brings life.

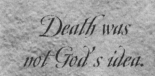

*Death was
not God's idea.*

God is life.[20]

FROM DIGNITY TO SHAME

Since the Fall, three fundamental traits have plagued
the human race. These contaminants have polluted the innate
consciousness of men and women, attesting to the far-reaching
effects of sin.

*Then the eyes of both of them were opened, and they knew
that they were naked.*[21]

Sin's first fingerprint upon the human creation was
shame. When Adam and Eve were separated from God's life,
the dignity with which they had been endowed was lost, and

---

19. I John 5:12 (NRSV)   20. John 1:4; 5:26; 6:63   21. Genesis 3:7

the long, dark shadow of humiliation and shame was cast across their lives. Adam and Eve had lived in the Garden of Eden with God in a magnificent relationship of love and trust. They had not experienced embarrassment, indignity, or disgrace. They were at home in God's glorious presence, with no consciousness of deficiency or of shame.[22]

Sin's first fingerprint upon the human creation was shame.

Anywhere or any time that people are separated from the light and life of God's sustaining presence, their human limitations become evident. They see themselves as naked, frail, vulnerable, and they are intuitively ashamed.

The deep-seated human disease of shame plagues people of all social classes and cultures. Persons without God are vulnerable to every negative influence that menaces and manipulates them. They hide in the darkness of night, cringing from the light, secretly committing their evil deeds, knowing that something is wrong. Separated from God, their unnatural sense of guilt and shame becomes the norm.

Human persons were created by God to live in dignity

---

22. Genesis 2:26

rather than in shame. Endowed with His own image and likeness, no human being was ever intended to grovel or to be debased. *God's Big Picture* exposes the wounds of sin so that there can be healing and wholeness again.

FROM EQUALITY TO SEPARATION

And they sewed fig leaves together and made themselves coverings.[23]

The second fingerprint of sin was *separation*—between God and people, and within the human family. Remember that Adam and Eve were created as an expression of God in the beginning. Their one flesh relationship with each other was a beautiful reflection of the oneness of God's person in whose image they were created. The human person was created to exist within that harmonious

As sin obstructed God's life-flow to Adam and Eve, everything changed.

interdependence. Sin slashed through the relationship between the Creator and His human family, causing the terrible cleavage

---

23. Genesis 3:7

In the beginning, God created people to have fellowship with each other and with Him.

that exists in human relationships today. As sin interdicted God's life-flow to Adam and Eve, everything changed. No longer one with their Creator, neither were they one with each other.

The sewn fig leaves symbolize both the *shame* and the *separation* that was engendered between Adam and Eve—and in the generations that followed. Human relationship was intended to be a reflection of the rapport that existed between people and God. When that seminal kinship was severed, it became impossible for people to experience mutually sustaining concord with each other.

People were created as social beings to have fellowship with God and with each other. People were designed to live together in community and harmony, as a reflection of their union with God. Because of sin, people became *alienated from the life of God.*[24] Consequently, they have erected between themselves psychological and cultural walls of distrust and suspicion that have estranged themselves from others.

24. Ephesians 4:18

Loneliness and isolation have become common human ills. They result from the separation of people from their Creator. Murder, abuse, jealousy, and envy remind us that without the unifying life of God, we can never experience oneness with others.

FROM PURPOSE TO FEAR

And they heard the sound of the LORD God walking in the garden in the cool of the day, and Adam and his wife hid themselves from the presence of the LORD God among the trees of the garden. Then the LORD God called to Adam and said to him, Where are you? So he said, I heard Your voice in the garden, and I was afraid because I was naked; and I hid myself.[25]

The third fingerprint of sin branded humanity with a deep, irrational *fear*. Separated from God, Adam and Eve became afraid of their Creator. Why? Their attitude of distrust led them to disobedience. Before that, they were not afraid of God. They walked and communed with Him. However, sin severed the connection of God's life-flow, leaving Adam and Eve alone and in death's shadow, filled with fear. Their created purpose to represent God was replaced with a terrifying sense

---

25. Genesis 3:8-10

of insecurity and fear. When people are afraid of God, they become afraid of each other. Fear is the primary motivation behind many of the evils that are committed by people. Much of the rage that burns in the human heart is a result of deep-seated fear.

> *When people are afraid of God, they become afraid of each other.*

People of almost every religion that I have encountered fear the god or the gods that they worship. The scars of sin have distorted their perceptions. Even many Christians live in trepidation, lest they do or say something that they fear may offend God. They do not know the root cause of their fear, nor do they understand how they can have a restored relationship with God. When reconciled to Him, their fear is replaced with confidence in God-given acceptance.

We were not created to live in fear. *For God has not given us a spirit of fear, but of power and of love and of a sound mind.*[26] Separation from God results in vulnerability to the ongoing deception of Satan. He *is a liar and the father of it.*[27]

26. 2 Timothy 1:7   27. John 8:44

ISOLATION'S LONG SHADOW

Satan's deception and Adam and Eve's sin so
completely altered the human condition that, without God's
initiative and intervention, there was no hope. In the Old
Testament the ancient patriarch, Job, describes the sad and

hopeless state
of humankind
separated from
their Creator.

*People without God
are vulnerable to the enemy.*

*Now my
days are swifter than
a runner; they flee away, they see no good. They pass by like swift ships,
like an eagle swooping on its prey. If I say, 'I will forget my complaint,
I will put off my sad face and wear a smile,' I am afraid of all my
sufferings; I know that You will not hold me innocent.*

*If I am condemned, why then do I labor in vain? If I wash
myself with snow water, and cleanse my hands with [lye] soap, yet
You will plunge me into the pit, and my own clothes will abhor me.
For He [God] is not a man, as I am, that I may answer Him, and
that we should go to court together. Nor is there any mediator between*

us, who may lay his hand on us both.[28]

Here, Job is describing the plight of people estranged from God. He articulates the groanings of the universal human spirit that is crying out, "What can I do? I have no hope.

All human attempts to reconnect with God are in vain.

Nothing that I do is good enough. I am guilty and I know it. I could scrub my hands until they bleed, but still they would not be clean."

In the New Testament, the Apostle Paul reiterates the condemned status of people separated from God by their sins and their iniquities.[29]

Remember that you were at that time separated (living apart) from … Him; utterly estranged and outlawed ... strangers with no share in the sacred compacts of the [Messianic] promise—with no knowledge of or right in God's agreements, His covenants. And you had no hope—no promise; you were in the world without God.[30]

People estranged from God are on a continual quest to find and to appease Him, whether or not they are conscious of their search. They often perform penance, or indulge in self-flagellation, some crawling on bloodied knees for miles

28. Job 9:25-33   29. Isaiah 59:2   30. Ephesians 2:12 (The Amplified Bible)

toward shrines and empty altars. All human attempts to reconcile with God are in vain. Nothing that an individual can do will ever bridge sin's separating chasm. The Apostle Paul asks the question that is within the heart of every person who is aware of his or her hopeless condition.

O wretched man that I am! Who will deliver me from this body of death?[31]

His answer gives hope to all people.

I thank God—through Jesus Christ our Lord![32] The only answer is in Him.

GOD'S DECLARATION OF LOVE

In the Garden of Eden, immediately after Adam and Eve turned from God in distrust and became trapped in the darkness of sin's *shame, separation, and fear,* God lifted His voice against Satan (hiding behind the serpent) and promised that a Redeemer would come to restore fallen humanity to their rightful place with Him.

So the Lord God said to the serpent, Because you have done this…on your belly you shall go, and you shall eat dust all the days of your life. And I will put enmity between you and the woman, and

---

between your seed and her Seed; He shall bruise your head, and you

shall bruise His heel.[33]

Satan's

deception

God lifted His voice
against Satan and promised
humanity's redemption.

dealt a

deathblow

to humanity.

However,

the enemy did not anticipate the immense love of God for

His creation.

What did God do? How did He traverse the chasm

of sin that separated Him from fallen humanity? What event

shifts our focus from the hopelessness of the human condition,

to the wonder of God's demonstrated love for people? How

did He intervene, restoring beauty, color, and splendor to

God's Big Picture?

33. Genesis 3:15

SCENE THREE
Christ's Substitution

*A light bursts
upon the canvas of
God's Big Picture,*

lifting our gaze from

the darkness and gloom

of human enslavement

through Satan's deception.

he Master Artist begins revealing an underlying scene that was sketched into place long before the destructive fingerprints of death smeared God's beautiful design.

Thousands of years had passed since the first and second scenes of *God's Big Picture* were revealed. Had the ugly strokes of deception irreparably marred the divine dream for humanity? Was the image damaged beyond repair? If not, who could restore the splendor of the garden scene and remove the blighting stain that had spread across the canvas of the beautiful world created by God? Only the eternal God could be both Master Artist and Master Restorer.

In His sovereign foresight, God had planned for the restoration of His masterpiece.[1] *Christ's substitution* was the answer. God would step out of the heavenly realm and would be incarnated in the flesh of a human being. As the sinless God-Man—Jesus Christ—He would take on Himself the sins of the whole world and would bear the penalty of humanity's transgression, thus removing the barrier that had separated people from God.[2]

---

1. Revelation 13:8   2. See John 1:1-4,14; Ephesians 1:7; Colossians 1:13-14; Hebrews 4:15; 1 Peter 2:24; 1 John 2:2

HUMAN DILEMMA

*At that time you were without Christ, being aliens …
having no hope and without God in the world.*[3]

Contemplating *God's Big Picture* of redemption,
one must remember that sin in the human family produced
a terrible harvest.
Its penalty was death.[4]
Because all persons
were guilty of sin,
and all were under
the judgment of death,
no human person could intervene on behalf of the guilty to bear
the punishment for their crime.[5]

*People were helpless
to redeem themselves.*

No degree of human goodness is adequate for
redemption.[6] Intellectual development cannot alter the human
condition. Moral behavior cannot reverse the effects of sin.

The Old Testament Law and the Levitical system of
atoning animal sacrifices were never intended to effectuate the
remission of sin—redemption.[7] They were God's illustrations
to expose human frailty, to reveal fallen humanity's inclination

---

3. Ephesians 2:12   4. Ezekiel 18:20; Romans 5:12, 6:23   5. Isaiah 59:15-17
6. Ephesians 2:8-9; Titus 3:5   7. Galatians 3:24; Hebrews 10:8,11

toward sin, and to foreshadow His coming in Christ to be the *once and for all* sacrifice for the sins of the world.[8]

Alienated from God, people were helpless to redeem themselves. No amount of human effort and goodness could effect salvation. God took the initiative to redeem humanity, motivated only by His love for those whom He had created.[9]

GOD'S INITIATIVE

For God so loved the world that He gave His only begotten Son, that whoever believes in Him should not perish but have everlasting life.[10]

But God demonstrates His own love toward us, in that while we were still sinners, Christ died for us.[11]

God accomplishes, through His initiating acts of love on our behalf, what we cannot achieve through our most ingenious attempts at self-transformation. It is vital to remember that we did not come to God; God came to us. We did not find Him; He found us. We did not believe first in God; God believed first in us. We did not love Him; He loved us. We did not bring our lives to God; He brought His life to us.

---

8. See Romans 5:20, 8:3-4; Galatians 2:16, 3:11,19; Hebrews 10:12-17
9. Romans 5:6; 1 John 4:10   10. John 3:16   11. Romans 5:8

God's love initiated our redemption; out of our need we respond to His rescue. We must never forget that God is the initiator of redemption, and that people only need to respond to His offer.

The third scene of *God's Big Picture* is a

God's love initiated our redemption; out of our need we respond to His rescue.

montage of several components that, together, form the beautiful portrait of Jesus Christ, our Redeemer.[12] The gospel—*God's Big Picture*—is more than a word. It is the central concept of God's eternal plan made visible in Christ. He, whose coming was prophesied throughout the Old Testament,[13] was born at the precise time that God had promised through His prophets.[14] He came as a baby, born of the Virgin Mary, and the wonder of His birth brought joy to those who recognized Him as the Messiah.[15]

---

12. Hebrews 12:2   13. See Isaiah 7:14, 9:1-7, 42:6; Luke 1:31-33, 67-75
14. Micah 5:2; Galatians 4:1-5   15. Luke 1:26-2:38

CHRIST'S LIFE
BECOMES HUMANITY'S HOPE

...God was in Christ, reconciling the world to Himself...[16]

When the eternal Master Artist could have simply destroyed the canvas and started over again, He lifted His palette and brush and lovingly began to restore beauty to the human scene. He mixed the only color that could obliterate the harshness of death-gray—the red of His own blood.[17]

The incarnation of God in Christ was a fusion of Deity with humanity.

The incarnation of God in Christ was a fusion of Deity with humanity. This perfect union—although sometimes difficult to comprehend—was necessary to accomplish the redemption of humankind. It was essential that Christ be fully human, so that He could bear the full punishment of our sin, as our substitute.[18] It was equally essential for Christ to be fully God, for only God had the power to forgive sin and to declare people "not guilty."[19]

---

16. 2 Corinthians 5:19   17. 1 Peter 1:8   18. Hebrews 2:14
19. See Psalm 86:5; Matthew 9:6; Luke 5:21; Acts 5:38-39; 1 John 1:9

3

In His earthly walk, Jesus demonstrated how men and women are to live while on this earth. He succeeded where Adam and Eve had failed.[20] He lived a perfect life, resistant to sin, consistent in His fellowship with the Father, and persistent in His mission to fulfill God's plan.[21]

Jesus was the supreme example of God's original dream to be expressed in human flesh. It was not flesh that marred the image of God

God came as a human person... affirming our humanity.

in humanity. It was sin that severed the relationship between God and people. God came as a human person, in flesh, thus affirming our flesh-wrapped humanity.

Christ's earthly life incarnates God's dream for human persons to live free from the bondage of sin, to express the authority of God over every adversity, to experience continual fellowship with the Creator, and to represent Him through their lives and influence. Jesus, as both God and man, was completely qualified to deal with the issue of sin, and to reveal the purpose of human existence.

---

20. 1 Peter 2:21-22; Hebrews 4:15
21. See Matthew 3:17; John 4:34, 5:30, 8:20; Philippians 2:8

CHRIST'S DEATH OVERTURNS HUMANITY'S DEATH SENTENCE

...John saw Jesus coming toward him, and said,
Behold! The Lamb of God who takes away the sin of the world![22]

Jesus, humanity's only Savior, took upon Himself the sin of the whole world. When He sacrificed His own life on the cross, He bore the punishment for all of humanity's sin so that every man and woman could be totally redeemed and released from the bondage of death—isolation from God. He who was innocent took upon Himself the sin and the consequences that humankind deserved to bear. Jesus paid our debt.[23] He is the only Redeemer.

For [God] made Him who knew no sin to be sin for us,
that we might become the righteousness of God in Him.[24]

My father, Dr. T. L. Osborn, writes, "If someone who is innocent of sin would be willing to take the place of someone who is guilty, and assume full punishment for their sin, then the guilty one would be free and could be restored to friendship with God, as though no sin had ever been committed. This was God's idea."[25]

---

22. John 1:29   23. Luke 1:68; Galatians 3:13-14   24. 2 Corinthians 5:21
25. T.L. Osborn, *God's Love Plan* (Tulsa, OK: OSFO BOOKS, 1984) 85-86.

Christ's substitution is the indispensable—the
pivotal scene in *God's Big Picture*. Our eyes are drawn to
His passion for people, as His love is displayed for all to see.
Our minds are bewildered as we try in vain to understand the
drama of His cross. Our hearts are gripped by the horror of
our own condition and by the Creator's personal identification
with our death-sentence.

Christ was our substitute in death. When He gave
His life on the cross,
it was not because
He was guilty of any
wrong. He died as our
substitute, in our place.
We were guilty; He was

> *Christ was
> our substitute in death.*

innocent.[26] His blood was poured out to remove all evidence
of sin from us and to buy us back—to redeem us—from
death. We deserved to die, but Christ died in our place—as
our substitute—so that by enduring the sentence of our
death He could restore us to new life with God, .[27]

---

26. See Isaiah 53:4-5; Romans 4:25; 2 Corinthians 5:21; Hebrews 4:14-16, 7:26
27. See John 6:38-40; Romans 6:5-7; 2 Corinthians 5:22; Hebrews 2:9; 1 John 3:18

SATAN'S POWER–
DESTROYED

…For this purpose the Son of God was manifested, that He might destroy the works of the devil.[28]

Christ's substitution liberates us from bondage under the influence and tyranny of Satan. We were powerless to overcome the barrage of negative and destructive forces that dominated and oppressed us. Without God, we could not discern between truth and deception. Our meager attempts to live morally and ethically were constantly foiled. The Deceiver had gained the advantage over us and we had become his victims.

Without God, we could not discern between truth and deception.

Just as Christ had no need to be punished for sin, neither did He need to become victorious over Satan. As God, He had committed no sin. However, we were guilty of sin;

---

28. 1 John 3:8

we were in bondage to Satan. God in Christ conquered

Satan in our name—on our behalf.[29]

Everyone who believes in Christ's substitutionary

death—His death on our behalf—is released from the rule of

sin and death, is rescued from the deceptive dominion of

Satan, and is restored to fellowship with God.[30]

CHRIST'S LIFE—
TRIUMPHANT

For I delivered to you first of all that which I also received:
that Christ died for our sins according to the Scriptures, and that
He was buried, and that He rose again the third day according to
the Scriptures.[31]

O Death, where is your sting? O Hades, where is your
victory? The sting of death is sin, and the strength of sin is the
law. But thanks be to God, who gives us the victory through our
Lord Jesus Christ.[32]

A burst of brilliant, iridescent color splashes across

God's Big Picture in a triumphal display of victory. *Christ's*

substitution did not end at the cross, and He did not remain

in the grave. Three days after His death and burial, God

---

29. John 1:1-5,14,16; 1 John 3:8   30. See Colossians 1:13-14, 2:11-15; Hebrews 2:14-15;
Revelation 5:9   31. 1 Corinthians 15:3-4   32. 1 Corinthians 15:55-57

raised Him from the dead. He came out of the tomb with all power and all authority. He tasted death on our behalf, conquered it for us, and now holds the keys of death, hell, and the grave.[33] Death—separation from God—is no longer our master.

The reality of Christ's resurrection is *the* distinctive of the Christian faith and the seal of our redemption.[34] The hallmark of the apostles' doctrine in the New Testament was Christ's resurrection.[35] They knew and proclaimed that Jesus is not dead; He is alive![36]

Christ's resurrection is the distinctive of the Christian faith.

In Christ's substitutionary death, burial, and resurrection, He dismissed our sin,[37] He defeated our adversary,[38] and He destroyed our death—our separation from God.[39]

---

33. See Matthew 28:18; Acts 2:24; Hebrews 2:14-15; Revelation 1:18
34. 1 Corinthians 15:13-17
35. See Acts 1:22, 2:31, 4:2, 33; 1 Corinthians 15:1-21
36. Hebrews 13:8
37. See Romans 6:6, 14; Colossians 2:13-14; Hebrews 10:15-22
38. See Luke 10:17-19; Colossians 2:10,15; Hebrews 2:14-18; James 4:7
39. See Isaiah 59:2; Matthew 27:51; Romans 8:1-2; Ephesians 2:14-18; Colossians 1:18; 1 Peter 3:18; Revelation 1:18

SHAME YIELDS
TO FORGIVENESS

In [Christ] we have redemption through His blood, the forgiveness of sins, according to the riches of His grace which He made to abound toward us...[40]

The shame that clouded the consciousness of people who were made in the image and likeness of God could at last be replaced by *forgiveness*. Humanity was not created to live in shame, to experience the weight of guilt, or to succumb to inferiority and worthlessness.

SEPARATION SURRENDERS
TO RELATIONSHIP

But now, in Christ Jesus, you who once were far off have been brought near by the blood of Christ.[41]

The separation between the Creator and His creation that had left people isolated from God, and that had deeply fractured the human family could finally be replaced by *relationship*. People were not created to endure the injustice

---

40. Ephesians 1:7-8   41. Ephesians 2:13

and cruelty of inequity. Human persons were never intended to be categorized according to gender, skin color, social and academic level, or any other societal distinctive. They were created to be in beautiful and intimate relationship with their Heavenly Father, and to enjoy unbroken fellowship and oneness with each other.[42] Everything that God determines for His children flows out of the relationship that they have with Him. The beautiful garden of relationship with God is recreated in the hearts of those who believe in Jesus Christ. God's paradise of love is restored.

> *People were not created to endure the injustice and cruelty of inequity.*

---

42. Colossians 1:19-22

FEAR IS OVERCOME
BY PEACE

Jesus said, These things I have spoken to you, that in Me you may have peace. In the world you will have tribulation; but be of good cheer I have overcome the world.[43]

People were not created to live in fear of God, of others, nor of themselves. Rather, the fear that once determined human attitudes and actions can now be replaced by the calming peace of God's loving presence.

The angels announced Christ's birth, singing, *Glory to God in the highest heaven, and on earth peace among those whom he favors!*[44] Because of *Christ's substitution,* we now have peace with God.[45] There is no need for fear and conflict. The good news of what Christ accomplished on our behalf through His death, burial and resurrection, constitutes the message that brings hope to humanity.[46] People were never created to live in bondage to shame, to separation, or to fear.

Etched against the horizon of *God's Big Picture,* the cross of Jesus Christ remains the eternal monument to His unconditional love for humankind, to their incalculable value to Him, and to their unquestionable liberty to return to Him.

---

43. John 16:33   44. Luke 2:14 (NRSV)   45. Romans 5:1   46. 1 Corinthians 1:18

This poem expresses the agony and the triumph of *Christ's substitution* that accomplished His redemptive mission to save us:

POEM BY E.W. KENYON

I stood one night on Calvary's height,
    where hung the Son of man,
I raised my eyes to starry skies,
    and mused on redemption's plan,
I saw the Fall, sin's bitter thrall,
    where plunged the human race,
I heard the moan that stirred the throne
    and moved the heart of grace,

I saw the Son, the spotless One,
    come from the Father's side,
In form prepared, our nature shared,
    and for the sinner died,
I saw the tree, He died for me,
    forsaken by His God,
I saw the blood, the crimson flood,
    dripping upon the sod,

I heard His cry that pierced the sky,
     the sad wail of the lost,
'My God, My God,' He kissed the rod,
     and paid sin's awful cost,
I heard the wail as men turned pale,
     the earth reeled at the stroke,
Sin's work was done, it slew the Son,
     its billows for Him broke,

His soul travail doth now prevail,
     our penalty is borne,
Hell feels His might, yields Him the fight,
     on resurrection morn,
I heard Him say, 'Go tell today,
     the Good News to the race,'
By God's decree, we all are free,
     saved by the Father's grace!"[47]

The brush of the Master Artist was not laid down because *God's Big Picture* was not yet complete. The final unfolding scene reveals the intimacy of restored communion between the Creator and the Creatures for whom He paid the ransom to redeem to Himself.

---

47. E.W. Kenyon, *The Father and His Family* (Seattle: Kenyon's Gospel Publishing Society, 1964) 130-1.

SCENE FOUR
Our Restoration

The unfolding artistry of
God's Big Picture

was first projected
in the Garden of Eden,

but then distorted
through the Fall of humanity.

It was restructured
at the Cross of Christ, and finally

is incarnated in the
flesh and blood of whoever
believes the gospel.

*T*he fourth scene of *God's Big Picture* of redemption depicts the greatest miracle of all. Human persons are *restored* to God as His friends and representatives, and are able to stand before Him without the sense of shame, guilt, condemnation, or inferiority—redeemed, reconciled, regenerated, and reborn to new and purposeful living.

How is this possible? When does the miracle begin? What is a person's responsive action that allows God's power to change …

> the marred to the mended,
>
> the corrupted to the converted,
>
> the sentenced to the saved, and
>
> the ruined to the redeemed?

WE PARTICIPATE IN THE MIRACLE

Trusting God and His plan to fully redeem humanity is the vital link between our old way of existence and our new life of experience with God. Just as Adam and Eve's choice to doubt God's integrity led them to disobey Him and to become estranged from Him, trusting God's redemptive work through Christ leads to our choice to obey God and to be restored to Him. We participate in our restoration by believing the gospel—by having faith in God and trusting His word.

The prerequisite of trust was brushed in graphic detail into the first scene of *God's Big Picture*. Understanding His original creation, prepares us to comprehend our present restoration.

In the Garden of Eden, trust, or faith, was the cohesive

> *We participate in our restoration by believing the gospel, by having faith in God.*

element in the relationship between God and the couple He created. When Adam and Eve doubted Him by questioning His word, their action annulled their relationship with Him. Questioning God's Word was sin and it resulted in their separation from Him. The penalty of sin was spiritual, physical, and eternal death—separation from their Creator.

God did not leave humanity in this fractured state. He came in the Person of Jesus Christ to redeem all humans, by taking on Himself their sins and by enduring the penalty of their transgressions. This substitutionary action—Christ dying in the place of those who were sentenced to death—purged, or expunged the sin that separated people from God. In *Christ's substitution*, everything that isolated humanity from God was removed, and all who were formerly condemned by sin were declared "not guilty."[1] This is the good news of Christ's glorious gospel.

FAITH—OUR RESPONSE TO GOD'S INITIATIVE

Without faith it is impossible to please God, for whoever would approach Him must believe that He exists and that He rewards those who seek Him.[2]

The fourth scene of *God's Big Picture* portrays the transformation that occurs when people hear and believe the good news of His rescue plan. Just as trust was required in the beginning, trust is required today.

> *Just as trust was required in the Garden of Eden, trust is required now.*

The Creation, the Fall, and the Cross are historic

---

1. Romans 3:24; 5:9 (The Living Bible)   2. Hebrews 11:6 (NRSV)

events recorded in Sacred Scripture. Christian believers must accept them as true, by faith.[3] There are myriad proofs of the validity of Scripture and of the truthfulness of the claims of Christ. However, we can never depend solely on empirical evidence to substantiate our faith in God. Individually, we must believe that He exists and that He rewards those who seek (or respond to) Him.

The only condition for our salvation is that we trust God and believe that what

God's love initiated our redemption; our faith responds to His love.

He accomplished for us in Jesus Christ is sufficient for our total restoration to Him.[4] No one can make this decision for us; we must each choose to believe in Jesus for our own salvation.

God's love initiated our redemption and makes it available as a gift of grace.[5] We respond to His love through our faith in His word. What He intended in the beginning can now be a living reality, in flesh and blood, in the lives of every person who believes the gospel.[6]

---

3. Hebrews 11:6   4. Acts 10:43, 16:31; Hebrews 11:6   5. Ephesians 2:8
6. Romans 10:9-13

WHAT HAPPENS WHEN
WE ARE RECONNECTED TO GOD?

God's original garden-blueprint for His human family is both the creation model and the restoration miracle. When we reflect on the garden pattern and remember what Christ accomplished on our behalf, we can understand the *restoration* that is our heritage as children of God. This marvelous trans-formation is not a future expectation. It is available as a present experience.[7]

Christianity is not simply a doctrinally-based way of thinking. Christianity is a Christ-based way of living. Our restoration is realized as, through faith in Christ, we are reunited to God. That re-union alters our entire worldview, value system and lifestyle. We become Christ-conscious. That is why we are called Christians.

> *Christianity is a Person-based way of living.*

If our restored relationship with God, through Christ,

---

7. 2 Corinthians 6:2

does not reshape our lifestyles, then our faith is no more than a religious philosophy or a future hope, without present significance.

Jesus answered ... Those who love me will keep my word, and my Father will love them, and we will come to them and make our home with them.[8]

The essential result of redemption is the restoration of relationship between God and people. To

This garden relationship is restored through Jesus Christ.

grasp the immensity of this redemptive blessing we must remember God's relationship-pattern in the beginning: He fashioned Adam from the dust of the ground; He breathed His own life into this newly formed creation; He animated humanity with His own breath, or Spirit. Then He walked with Adam and Eve in the garden, in the cool of the day.[9] When they violated the trust that He placed in them, this intimate relationship—this God-presence—was lost to them.

Redemption is more than the forgiveness of sin; it is the re-impartation of God's life in us.[10] This is our new beginning; we have a new identity; we are born again.[11] God's life that

---

8. John 14:23 (NRSV)   9. Genesis 2:7, 3:8   10. John 10:10   11. John 3:3-17

was in Christ is now miraculously imparted into us when we believe His word.

Everything that God wills for humanity flows out of the relationship that unites Him with people. Everything that concerns our lives changes when we discover a personal relationship with God, through Christ. The sin that separated us from Him is expunged.[12] We have peace with God; we are no longer alienated from Him.[13] We can now walk with Him and know His voice.[14] This garden relationship, this union of divinity and humanity, is restored through Jesus Christ.

When we perceive *God's Big Picture* and embrace it, our restoration begins. The three principal consequences of sin in human persons—shame, separation, and fear—are reversed.

HUMAN DIGNITY—
RESTORED

The dignity that God intends for humanity created in His own image is often difficult to comprehend. Some Bible scholars believe that the relationship between God and people is the image of God in human persons. Others argue that the

---

12. See Psalm 103:12; Romans 3:24; Titus 2:14; Colossians 1:14, 21-22; 1 Peter 2:24-25, 3:18; Romans 5:10   13. Romans 5:1,10; Colossians 1:19-22   14. Ephesians 5:8

image of God in people is something that they do, a function that they perform. However, the gospel of redemption—*God's Big Picture*—makes it clear that the image of God is not what we have, or what we do, but it is what we are because of what He has done.[15]

The image of God was so distorted and marred by sin that the positive motivation behind every human decision became corrupted.[16] The image of God within humanity degenerated to a residue

Our restoration includes the recovery of God's image in us.

of shame that infected every human thought and action.

The good news is that our restoration includes the recovery of God's image in us. When a person believes the gospel and is restored to God, he or she begins the process of being conformed (or re-formed) to one's original image.[17] Shame no longer contaminates the subconscious, causing men and women to react from a distorted and inferior self-image. Our restoration means that we can be free from the sinful motivations that influence unconverted lives.

Behold what manner of love the father has bestowed on us,

that we should be called children of God![18]

As children of God, we are restored to our created status as God's royal offspring. His identity once again becomes our identity.[19] We become members of His family.[20] Our inheritance is among those who also believe in Christ.[21] We no longer live under condemnation and guilt.[22] We are redeemed. Our dignity is restored.

The infinite price that was paid by Christ to redeem us is the exact measure of our value to God.[23] Human dignity is our birthright. No longer do we listen to influences that suggest that we are not valuable, that our lives have no meaning, or that we are insignificant. *Our restoration* in Christ means the removal of our shame and the restoration of our God-ordained dignity as human persons.

DESTINED EQUALITY– REKINDLED

In God's garden-pattern, Adam and Eve represented all of humanity. They were both created in God's image and likeness.[24] God blessed both of His human offspring.[25]

The separation between God and His creation that

---

19. Galatians 2:20   20. Romans 8:15   21. Acts 26:18; Ephesians 3:14-15; 1 Peter 2:9
22. Romans 8:1   23. 1 Peter 1:18-19   24. Genesis 1:27   25. Genesis 1:28

resulted from sin, spawned division throughout the human family. That separation has been expressed throughout human history by wars, injustice, and all manner of cruelty among people.

After the Fall, God prophesied to Eve that her husband would begin to rule over her.[26] That consequence of sin continues to influence social norms in every culture of the world. Inequity was never intended as the pattern for male-female behavior. Sin's separation shattered the beautiful partnership between Adam and Eve.

In many tribal cultures today, women are considered to be of little more value than animals. In more sophisticated societies, gender inequity is subtler, but nevertheless pervasive and debilitating.

Even in the Christian world, deeply entrenched bias against women—the result of sin—continues to influence interpretations of Bible verses, and to perpetuate archaic and debasing attitudes and decisions concerning the roles of Christian women.

This sin-rooted disease of social fragmentation has divided races, cultures, tribes, and families. The male/female polarization has caused the most consistently imposed, and

---

26. Genesis 3:16

the most cruelly inflicted injustices against women everywhere.

The clarity of *God's Big Picture* allows us to see that the original plan for human equality was disrupted by sin. However, God's redemptive work in Christ makes it possible for the human family to be restored to their created and lofty position as one united community of equals, reflecting the oneness of their Creator.

Before Jesus' death, in His prayer for us, He said, *I do not pray for these alone, but also for those who will believe in Me through their word; that they all may be one as You, Father, are in Me, and I in You, that they also may be one in Us, that the world may believe that You sent Me.*[27]

Men and women can be reunited in harmonious and mutually dependent relationships.

The awe inspiring fourth scene of *God's Big Picture* reveals the restoration of His plan as He intended it to be in the beginning. Christ removed the sin that separated people from God, and from each other.

Our restoration means that men and women—all

27. John 17:20-21

people—can be reunited with each other in harmonious and interdependent relationships.

> *For in Christ Jesus you are all children of God through faith. As many of you as are baptized into Christ have clothed yourselves with Christ. There is no longer Jew or Greek, there is no longer slave or free, there is no longer male and female, for all of you are one in Christ Jesus.*[28]

Since all who have experienced the miracle of God's salvation are now in Christ,[29] and because His life is in all who believe the gospel,[30] there is no longer any legitimate separation of people from God or from each other.[31]

Our restoration, through the power of the gospel, mends the brokenness that has plagued society since humanity's separation from God's presence. Now, men and women, rich and poor, educated and illiterate, people of all racial, ethnic, and cultural differences can find their new identity—their predestined equality—in Jesus Christ and can be reunited with each other on that common ground of faith and trust in Him.

---

28. Galatians 3:26-28 (NRSV)   29. 2 Corinthians 5:17   30. John 14:23
31. Ephesians 2:14-18

DIVINE PURPOSE–
RENEWED

In the beginning, God's plan for His human creation included a divine purpose. He instructed Adam and Eve to be fruitful and to multiply, to populate the earth with Godlike creatures.[32]

The biblical mandate to multiply and replenish the earth has often been interpreted as simply an edict to procreate.[33] However, the full panorama of *God's Big Picture* elevates human purpose beyond animal instinct for the preservation of the species.

The gospel is the good news of God's miraculous restoration of humankind to His creational purpose. What was that divine purpose? Many verses of Scripture in the New Testament cast light upon statements in chapters one and two of Genesis, which express humanity's created purpose.

Remember, God's plan was ordained in the beginning, thwarted by the Fall, and recovered by Christ. God's redemptive work in Christ is not a creation; it is the re-creation of God's

---

32. Genesis 1:28   33. Genesis 1:28

original plan. To understand *our restoration*, we review God's creation.

Jesus said, *I am the vine, you are the branches. Those who abide in me and I in them bear much fruit, because apart from me you can do nothing. My Father is glorified by this, that you bear much fruit, and become my disciples. You did not choose me but I chose you. And I appointed you to go and bear fruit, fruit that will last, so that the Father will give you whatever you ask him in my name.*[34]

Just as God intended His human creation to reproduce Godlike creatures in the beginning, so He endows the Christian with the honorable purpose and mission to reproduce Godlike creatures—others who believe in Christ's gospel, and who become restored to the image of God in the earth.

So if anyone is in Christ, there is a new creation: everything old has passed away; see, everything has become new! All this is from God, who reconciled us to himself through Christ, and has given us the ministry of reconciliation; that is, in Christ God was reconciling the world to himself, not counting their trespasses against them, and entrusting the message of reconciliation to us.

So we are ambassadors for Christ, since God is making his appeal through us; we entreat you on behalf of Christ, be

---

34. John 15:5,8,16 (NRSV)

reconciled to God. For our sake he made him to be sin who knew no sin, so that in him we might become the righteousness of God.[35]

Just as God became flesh in Christ, so Christ becomes flesh in us. When God restores us to Himself through Christ, He renews our purpose as His representatives in the earth.

Just as God became flesh in Christ, so Christ becomes flesh in us.

We become His ambassadors of good news, inviting others to also come back to God. This was Christ's purpose; it is now our purpose. Christ's ministry of loving reconciliation continues through us.

The opportunity to reconcile people to God, and to each other, is the most awesome and life-changing calling that any person can experience.

Christ's life in us is love yearning to be expressed to others through forgiveness, healing, comfort, and relationship.[36] Every man or woman who believes in Christ is restored to the noble purpose of being a light in a world of darkness.[37]

God's Big Picture—the gospel—is the divine revelation that…

---

35. 2 Corinthians 5:19-21 (NRSV)　36. 2 Corinthians 5:14　37. Matthew 5:13-16

Redemption starts with God's plan;

Redemption is tested by separation;

Redemption is triumphant through Christ; and

Redemption is now entrusted to us.

Do you not know that you are the temple of God and that the Spirit of God dwells in you?[38]

Christ expresses Himself today through His people—His Church, or His Body—those who believe in Him. *The word [God] was made flesh* in Christ.[39] Now that same word is made flesh in believers. Our purpose is to continue the work of reconciliation that Christ began during His earthly ministry. This, in essence, is the ministry of the Church—the Body of Christ.

God made people for a purpose. That purpose is that they together be His dwelling place so that others who do not know Him *Christ can only express Himself today in the flesh of His people.* can hear His love-invitation—the gospel—and by believing it, they too can become reunited with Him.

38. 1 Corinthians 3:16   39. John 1:14

THE PICTURE–
REFOCUSED

With a clear perspective of *God's Big Picture*, suddenly our world looks different. It no longer appears threatening. Rather, we see it as our place for influence and for purposeful living. People no longer need to be feared or controlled. They are perceived as valued creations of God, to whom His love and redemptive power is to be expressed.

Redemption is the restoration of God's plan in and through His people. It is the reinstatement to, the recovery of, and the return to the Garden of Eden lifestyle, where the loving Creator and His beautiful human creatures are reunited in purposeful relationship.

WHERE DO WE GO FROM HERE?

What is the gospel? It includes four dynamic events that comprise God's plan. With a clear perception of these four facts, the Bible makes sense.

God's Creation is the starting point for understanding

and for communicating the gospel. The most ennobling and dignifying fact of history is to know that each human person is the offspring of God and that each one is created for a worthy and divine purpose.

Satan's Deception is an essential factor in the full scope of the gospel. The calamities, evils, and injustices in our world were not God's plan. Satan's cunning deception influenced Adam and Eve to doubt God, separating them from His life and enslaving humanity by Satan's death.

Christ's Substitution is God's love-initiative to reverse the human dilemma and is therefore the key to the gospel. God came in the Person of Christ to assume the guilt and to endure the punishment of humanity's sin, so that no judgment could ever again be imposed upon those who trust in Christ.

Our Restoration is the climax of the gospel. With the knowledge of God's Creation, of Satan's Deception, and of Christ's Substitution, people can comprehend why they can be restored to friendship with God and to purposeful and joyous living.

The miraculous truth revealed in the fourth scene of *God's Big Picture* is that God can live in people once again. Christ removed the sin that separated them from Him.

A person is reunited with God the moment that he or she hears the gospel and receives Christ by faith. This miracle, also called the new birth, is the impartation of Christ's life to those who believe in Him.[40] When we believe in Jesus Christ and are redeemed to God, His Spirit is again the life that animates us, restoring His image in the earth.[41]

> *Every person who is restored to God in Christ becomes the carrier of His life.*

Every person who is restored to God in Christ becomes the carrier of His life. Sin—the condition of death (or separation from God) is removed through Christ, making it possible for Him to come and live in and through people. This Christ-presence is a living reality in the biblical Christian.

Paul said, *I have been crucified with Christ; it is no longer I who live, but Christ lives in me; and the life which I now live in the flesh I live by faith in the Son of God, who loved me and gave Himself for me.*[42]

When Christ comes to live in people, the most liberating reality is established in them:

40. 1 John 5:12; 2 Corinthians 4:11, 6:16,18   41. John 20:21-22; 1 John 3:1-2
42. Galatians 2:20

His purpose becomes their purpose;

His will becomes their will;

His compassion becomes their compassion;

His energy becomes their energy;

His mind becomes their mind;

His passion becomes their passion;

His priorities become their priorities;

His nature becomes their nature;

His peace becomes their peace;

His status becomes their status; and

His LIFE becomes their LIFE.[43]

The greatest miracle of biblical Christian faith is that Christ comes to live in those who believe in Him, who receive Him, and who trust Him as their Savior and Lord.

[God is] *not willing that any should perish but that all should come to repentance.*[44]

Our faith in Christ—His life, His death, and His resurrection—allows God's miracle in us to begin. When we choose to believe the gospel, we are instantly released from the slavery of death, and restored to the liberty of life. The miracle of *our restoration* is the incarnation of *God's Big Picture*

---

43. 1 John 4:17   44. 2 Peter 3:9

in our flesh, as a living experience, rather than a lingering exhibit.

It is God's yearning desire for every person to hear and to embrace this good message.[45] In my imagination I can see God at the edge of the third gospel scene—the cross behind Him, our future before Him—His arms outstretched as He leans into the fourth gospel scene, beckoning us home to His garden of relationship, restoring us to Himself and to our divine purpose.

God beckons you to discover the unique you that He has created, and to see the wonder of your life as it unfolds and blossoms in His plan.

45. John 1:2, 6:37; Acts 2:21

Epilogue
FINDING YOURSELF IN GOD'S PLAN

*Now you see
God's Big Picture—the
panorama of His great plan.*

It began with
beautiful detail in Genesis,

it persisted through
the ugly, gray-death of the Fall,

it was brightened with color and hope
at the Cross,

and it continues its re-creative artistry
in the lives of people today who
hear and believe the gospel.

I am not ashamed of the Gospel of Christ, for it is the power of God to salvation for everyone who believes, for the Jew first and also for the Greek. For in it the righteousness of God is revealed from faith to faith; as it is written, 'The just shall live by faith.'[1]

This good news is for everyone, including you and including me.[2]

Step back and ponder the incomparable revelation of God's love—His plan—for you. Where are you in the scene? Are you living in any degree of shame because of events that have occurred in your life? Do you feel lonely, isolated or strangely separated from people even when surrounded by them? Are there fears that you cannot overcome, that limit areas of your life?

> *It is not God's plan for you to live in shame, in separation, or in fear.*

Remember, it is not God's plan for you to live in shame, in separation, or in fear. The purpose of this book is to lift your eyes and to help you to see how much God loves you and what an infinite price He paid to bring

1. Romans 1:16-17   2. John 1:12, 6:37; Acts 2:21

you home to Himself. Your life is of immeasurable value
to your loving Creator.

It has been my privilege to proclaim the Gospel of
Christ in nations around the world. The transforming power
of God has been experienced in the lives of people on every
continent, as they have heard and comprehended the good
news of God's plan.
No circumstance is
too difficult. No person
is too hopeless. No
problem is too complex.

*The Gospel is the answer
to every human need.*

No sickness is too advanced. No crime is too heinous. The
gospel is God's answer to every human need.

One story will illustrate the redeeming power of
God's love in action.

A woman by the name of Betty Andiru lived in
Uganda, East Africa during the rule of the tyrannical dictator,
President Idi Amin. Undisciplined and cruel soldiers, infected
by the brutality of their leader, burned villages, murdered at will,
raped women and girls without restraint, and in unimaginable
ways terrorized the Ugandans for many years. People who are
alienated from God will stoop lower than animals, committing

---

1 Revelation 13:8 2 See John 1:1-4, 14; Ephesians 1:7; Colossians 1:13-14;
Hebrews 4:5; I Peter 2:24; I John 2:2

cruel and violent acts against their fellow human beings.

One day soldiers came to Betty's village, stealing her from her family, and raping her repeatedly. They kept her as their prisoner, violating, inflicting pain, and dehumanizing her until finally, filled with rage, she lost her mind. A destructive, demonic spirit of hatred possessed her, and she began barking like a dog, lunging at her captors and snapping at them with her teeth. She was confined with chains, and was treated like a wild animal, eating whatever morsels were tossed within her reach. Betty's life was a graphic portrayal of the enemy's passion to destroy God's beautiful creation.

Following the collapse of Amin's brutal government, we went to Uganda to conduct a great Crusade of Bible Faith. The entire nation needed a vivid reminder of God's unfailing love toward them and of His plan to rescue them from the death-grip of Satan's bondage.

Each day, thousands of people believed in God's plan of salvation through Christ, and as they accepted Him into their lives, hundreds of physical healing miracles took place. Blind eyes were opened. Deaf ears were unstopped. Crippled legs were restored. The gospel is indeed the power of God to everyone who believes.[3]

---

3. Many of the miracles of healing reported during the Kampala, Uganda, Crusade of Bible Faith are documented in my parents' book, *The Gospel According to T.L. & Daisy*, Tulsa, Oklahoma: OSFO Publishers, 1986.

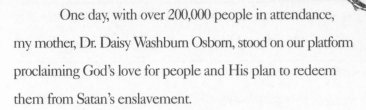

One day, with over 200,000 people in attendance, my mother, Dr. Daisy Washburn Osborn, stood on our platform proclaiming God's love for people and His plan to redeem them from Satan's enslavement.

The multitude was riveted to her words. Those oppressed Ugandans were grasping for new hope in God. They were like a field of dehydrated plants, frantically absorbing the Water of Life, as the words of God's love were poured out to them.

A Christian believer who knew of Betty's condition had brought her to the crusade. She was restrained at the edge of the enormous crowd, to minimize the disturbance of her continual barking. We could hear the noise during the meeting, but assumed that it was someone's dog.

After the message, the people were guided in accepting Jesus Christ as Savior, to become His followers. Thousands were converted that day. Then, those who were physically ill were asked to lay their hands on their own bodies, wherever they were suffering, while Dr. Daisy prayed a mass prayer for the multitude. She asked the Lord to show Himself alive by doing the same miracles that He did during His earthly ministry.

Remarkable miracles began to occur throughout the

immense crowd. Crutches, braces, and wheelchairs were
hoisted above the heads of the multitude, indicating that
lame people, cripples, and paralytics had begun walking.
Exuberant rejoicing swept through the enormous multitude
as people began exhibiting what Christ had done for them.

We welcomed those who were healed to the platform
to give public witness of Christ's miracle in their life. In minutes,
the platform was jammed with men, women, and children,
who had experienced a physical miracle.

A poor village woman made her way to the microphone
and began to speak. It was Betty, that dear woman who had
been dehumanized by brutal soldiers—the one who had been
barking. She was completely healed and her friends had
helped her through the crowd so the people could know of
the miracle that had taken place.

Betty was covered with dirt. Dried grass was mixed
in her hair. Her clothing was filthy and disheveled. It was
obvious that something remarkable had taken place. Her eyes
were beautiful and clear. To us, they looked like the eyes of
an angel. As she told her story, tears ran down her cheeks.

Betty told the people that hate had taken possession
of her as she plotted to avenge herself of those who had

brutalized and violated her body. Finally, her mind had snapped and she had become like a wounded, wild animal. She could not remember being brought to the crusade, but while Dr. Daisy's voice was heard over the loud speaker, something had happened. Betty had suddenly been restored to her right mind. The tormenting demons of destruction had left her. Hatred and revenge had been replaced by love and peace.

The multitude wept with Betty, as she related the terrible shame of her dehumanizing experience. They marveled at the miracle of God's love that had washed away the pain of her horrifying memories. God had restored her mind and had given her a new beginning in life.

Betty returned to her village and to her family. Thirteen years earlier, she had been promised in marriage to a good and decent man. To her amazement, he had waited for her. When the people in her village heard Betty's report of the gospel, and witnessed God's miracle that had restored her mind and heart, they believed on and accepted Christ. Betty and her newly converted Christian husband became living witnesses to the power of Christ's love in that region of Uganda.

I cannot explain how the miracle of restoration takes

place. Everywhere the Gospel of Jesus Christ is communicated to hurting people, He is there, expressing His resurrected life through miracles and loving restoration. Each wonder wrought is another proof that Jesus Christ is the same yesterday, today, and forever.[4]

Wherever I teach and preach the truths of the gospel—whether in Papua New Guinea, China, Russia, Zambia, or any other nation of the world—I emphasize God's creation and the Garden of Eden lifestyle that He intended for humanity. When people grasp the significance of God's original creation, they can understand how wondrous, how comprehensive, and how absolute is this "great salvation"[5] that is revealed in the Bible.

For He says: In an acceptable time I have heard you, and in the day of salvation I have helped you. Behold, now is the accepted time; behold, now is the day of salvation.[6]

At our headquarters church—International Gospel Center—in Tulsa, Oklahoma, a large banner is mounted in the sanctuary. It states four facts of Bible truth that embrace the essence of this book:

1. There is a God.
2. God has a plan.

---

4. Hebrews 13:8   5. Hebrews 2:3   6. 2 Corinthians 6:2

3. God's plan is working.

4. God's plan includes you.

Today, choose to believe that God's redemptive work in Christ includes *you*. Accept His love, His forgiveness, and His life. The moment that you believe the four fundamentals set forth in this book, God's miracle begins in you and two remarkable things happen in your life:

> *The moment that you believe, God's miracle begins in you.*

First, you are restored to God as His child, as though no sin had ever occurred in your life; you are incorporated into Christ's body. You stand before God, in Christ, free from all condemnation.[7]

Second, the life of Christ—His Spirit—begins to work in you, conforming you to the image of Christ.[8] This means that by the power of His presence in you, you become progressively like Christ in every way. As His life changes your lifestyle, you become a witness to others of His power to restore humanity according to God's plan.[9]

Just as you stand before God in Christ, so Christ

7. See Matthew 26:28; John 1:12; Romans 5:1, 8:1; 2 Corinthians 5:17, 21; Colossians 1:14; Hebrews 10:17; 1 Peter 5:7   8. Romans 8:29   9. See Psalms 37:23-24; Romans 8:37; 1 Corinthians 3:16-17; 2 Corinthians 6:16, 18; Galatians 2:20; Philippians 1:6; Colossians 1:27

stands before the world in you. This becomes your ennobling new identity and your divinely destined purpose.

Keep *God's Big Picture* focused in your mind. These four scenes show you His plan clearly, so that you can understand His love completely, and can experience His life personally.

Scene One of the gospel depicts God's beautiful dream and original plan for you, created in His own image and likeness, destined to live in fellowship and harmony with Him.

Scene Two details the deadly, destructive work of Satan that led to humanity's catastrophic separation from God's presence and which is the cause of all pain and suffering.

Scene Three portrays God's immeasurable love in giving His Son, Jesus Christ, to endure the punishment for your sins—in your place—redeeming you back to Himself as a member of His own family.

Scene Four reveals you in your new beginning, redeemed, ransomed, reconciled, and restored to God as His friend and partner in reconciling others to Him. You have been brought back into God's original plan.

As you comprehend and believe God's redemptive plan, it is as though you were never separated from Him. *God's Big Picture* is fulfilled. God's dream is restored.

Believe NOW—

and recognize yourself in

God's Big Picture.

THE INTERNATIONAL MINISTRY OF
LaDonna C. Osborn

LaDonna Osborn is Vice-President and CEO of Osborn International, the world missionary church established by her parents, T.L. and Daisy Osborn, over 50 years ago.

Today, the Osborn ministries share the gospel of Jesus Christ on every continent, reaching over 80 nations of the world through face-to-face evangelism and training, and through the distribution of gospel literature published in 132 languages.

Dr. LaDonna Osborn is founder and bishop of the International Gospel Center Fellowship of Churches and Ministries (IGCF), an international network of over 250 churches and ministries, headquartered at Tulsa, Oklahoma's International Gospel Center Church. She is a member of the College of Bishops for the International Communion of Charismatic Churches, which represents over 7,000 pastors, 9,000 churches and more than ten million believers worldwide.

Her international ministry reflects the two-fold commission of Christ to the Church: 1) evangelizing the unchurched, and 2) equipping the churched to become Christ's representatives in this world. Dr. Osborn's gospel influence is expressed through mass miracle evangelism, leaders, pastors, missions, and women's conferences, gospel literature distribution, the production of redemption-based teaching courses and through her training and oversight of the pastors and churches who participate in the IGC Fellowship. She is widely recognized and respected as an authority in world missions and church leadership.

LaDonna Osborn received her Bachelor of Arts (BA) degree from Oklahoma City University, her Master of Arts in Practical Theology (MA) degree from Oral Roberts University, and her Doctor of Ministry (D.Min.) degree from American Christian College and Seminary. Dr. Osborn has four children and 15 grandchildren. She and her husband live in Tulsa, Oklahoma.

MIRACLE EVANGELISM

Dr. LaDonna Osborn has been involved with her parents, T.L. and Daisy Osborn, on their platforms of world evangelism since she was a child. Her life is a living example of Christ's love for people, and she now carries the gospel into this century's new frontiers including China, Russia, French-speaking Africa and the ex-communist nations of Eurasia.

Everywhere that the gospel of Jesus Christ is proclaimed, His living power is demonstrated through countless testimonies of miraculous healing and deliverance.

LEADERS AND PASTORS CONFERENCES

Throughout the world, Dr. Osborn teaches men and women the successful ministry methods that have marked the Osborn ministry for over half a century.

In China, where open evangelism is prohibited, Dr. Osborn met five times daily for one week with key Chinese leaders, each of whom were supplied with the Mandarin translation of T.L. Osborn's book, *Healing the Sick*.

Dr. Osborn is committed to sharing the ministry knowledge that she has gained throughout her life, and to providing the tools leaders and pastors need for successful ministry.

WOMEN'S
CONFERENCES

Dr. LaDonna Osborn's
mother, Daisy Washburn Osborn
(left in photo) was a bold pioneer
for women's redemption rights to
obey Christ's commands.

Now her daughter continues to teach
at women's conferences throughout the world.
She is a living exampleof God's limitless power
expressed through a woman.

Above: Dr. Osborn presents
redemption teaching courses in Russian during
the first International Women's Conference in Russia
where delegates gathered from 212 regions, republics
and areas of the former Soviet Union.

As founder and bishop
of the International Gospel
Center Fellowship of Churches
and Ministries, Dr. Osborn
is actively involved in
the training and ordaining
of both women and men
into gospel ministry.

PUBLISHING
AND DISTRIBUTION

Dr. Osborn's redemption-based books
and teaching courses, audio and video materials,
along with gospel literature produced by
T.L. and Daisy Osborn, are distributed
by the ton worldwide to facilitate gospel
workers and to equip men and women
to do the work of the ministry.

These materials, in conjunction with
miracle crusades, are the seed that has
enabled the Osborn Ministries to effect change
and produce a broad harvest in nations
around the world.

Notes

BOOKS BY

OSBORN
PUBLISHERS

Believers in Action — *Apostolic-Rejuvenating*

Biblical Healing — *Seven Miracle Keys,*
4 Visions - 50+ Years of Proof - 324 Merged Bible Vs.

Five Choices for Women Who Win — *21st Century Options*

God's Big Picture — *An Impelling Gospel Classic*

God's Love Plan — *The Awesome Discovery*

Healing the Sick — *A Living Classic*

How to Be Born Again — *The Miracle Book*

Jesus & Women — *Big Questions Answered*

Life-Triumph Over Tragedy — *A True Story of Life After Death*

New Life for Women — *Reality Re-focused*

Soulwinning-Outside the Sanctuary —
A Classic on Biblical Christianity & Human Dignity

The Best of Life — *Seven Energizing Dynamics*

The Good Life — *A Mini-Bible School - 1,467 Ref.*

The Gospel, According to T.L. & Daisy —
Their Life & World Ministry - 510 pg. Pictorial

The Message that Works —
T.L.'s Revealing Manifesto on Biblical Faith

The Power of Positive Desire —
An Invigorating Faith Perspective

The Woman Believer — *Awareness of God's Design*

Woman Without Limits — *Unmuzzled-Unfettered-Unimpeded*

Women & Self-Esteem — *Divine Royalty Unrestrained*

You Are God's Best — *Transforming Life Discoveries*

Most Osborn books, audio or video cassettes are available
at quantity discounts for bulk purchases, to be used for
gifts, resale, ministry outreaches, education or other purposes.